SOLVING THE RIDDLE OF MICROSOFT AND YOUR COMPUTER

2ND EDITION

MARK RIDDLE

author HOUSE·

AuthorHouse™
1663 Liberty Drive
Bloomington, IN 47403
www.authorhouse.com
Phone: 833-262-8899

Published by AuthorHouse 11/02/2021

ISBN: 978-1-6655-4320-0 (sc)
ISBN: 978-1-6655-4319-4 (hc)
ISBN: 978-1-6655-4321-7 (e)

Library of Congress Control Number: 2021922309

Print information available on the last page.

Contents

1. Facts About Your Computer

Chapter one provides some useful facts about your computer. It describes such things as how to operate your mouse; how to modify your screen saver and printer settings; options for printing files; how to use different functions of the calculator; playing and storing music; using Snipping Tool to capture images; determining amount of Radom Access Memory (RAM) is on your computer; determining your computer name; how to use Microsoft Excel to keep track of financial transactions.

1.1 The Mouse.

The mouse is comprised of two parts, the left mouse and the right mouse. Figure 1.1 illustrates the left and right mouse.

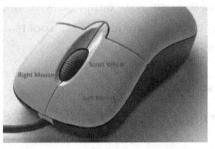

Figure 1.1 The Mouse

1.1.1 Left Mouse Functions.

The left mouse is the most commonly used part of the mouse. It is most frequently used to select items. Listed below are a few functions of the left mouse.

1.1.1.1 Selecting a Pull-down Menu.

For example, if you want to save a Microsoft Word file using the pull-down menu.

♦   Move your cursor until it is on top of the "File" pull-down menu.
♦   Click once on the left mouse.

- A pull-down menu will appear.
- Locate the save function and click the left mouse once.

1.1.1.2 Highlighting Text.

In many instances you will need to highlight text in the documents.

- Place the cursor next to the text you wish to highlight.
- Click and hold down the left mouse and pull to right.
- Once this is accomplished, you can modify the text to your hearts content.

1.1.1.3 Activating Toolbar Functions.

The left mouse is used to activate all toolbar functions such as save, print, left justify, bold and so forth. For example, to save an existing Microsoft application, simply click the save icon once. Tool bar functionality will be discussed in detail in a later section.

1.1.2 Right Mouse Functions.

1.1.2.1 Viewing Different Types of Applications Simultaneously.

This function enables you to view different types of applications at the same time. If you have Microsoft Word and Microsoft Power Point open at the same time, this mouse function enabled you to view both applications at the same time. One of the most important uses for this function is that you can copy from one application into the other application with ease. This function works with all applications even if they are not Microsoft products.

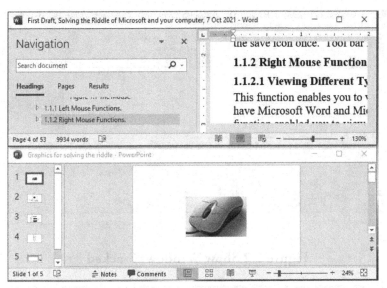

Figure 1.2 Viewing Different Applications
Simultaneously Stacked

♦ Open Microsoft Word and Microsoft Power Point. Normally the application toolbar is located on the bottom of your screen. It should look similar to Figure 1.2 above.

♦ Right click to the right of second (Microsoft Power Point) application.

♦ A pull-down menu appears as offering two options: Show windows Stacked or show windows side by side.

♦ The options to select from the pull-down menu (enclosed by a red border) are:

  ♦ Show windows Stacked – Figure 1-2.

  ♦ Show windows side by side – Figure 1-3.

♦ Left click the selection you desire. See Figures 1-2 and 1-3 illustrate the differences between the two options.

♦ When you have two different applications open, you can move back and forth simply by clicking on it. An active application is indicated by dark blue.

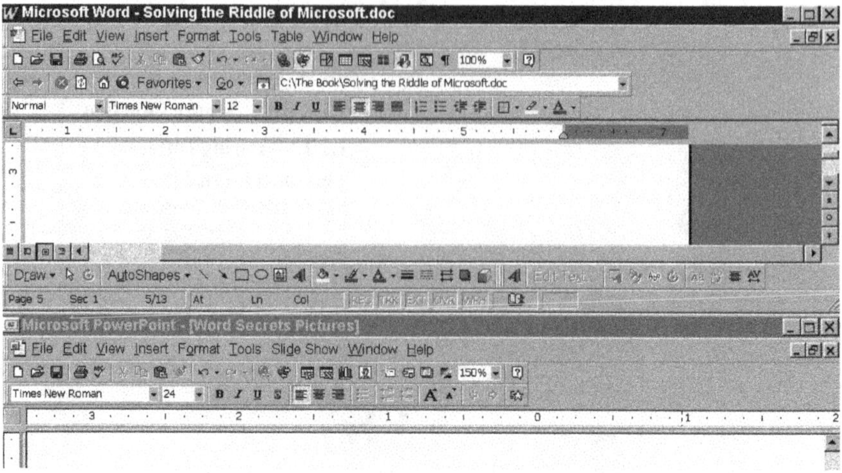

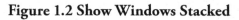

Figure 1.2 Show Windows Stacked

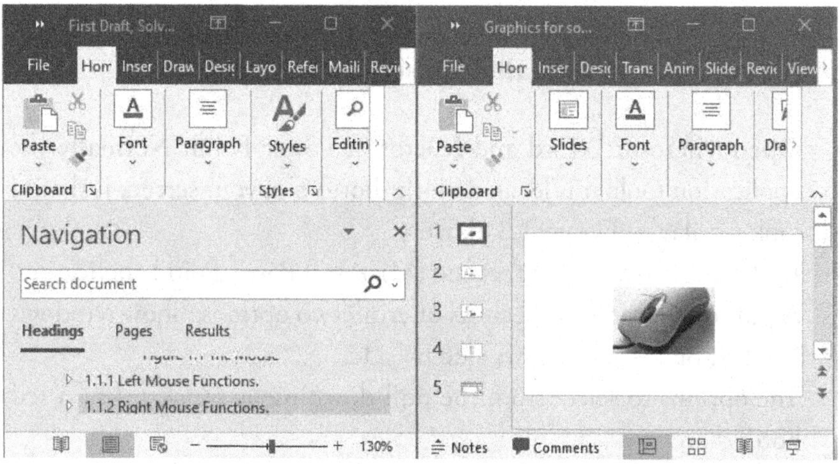

Figure 1.3 Show Windows Side by Side

1.2 Modifying Settings.

1.2.1 Modifying Your Screen Saver.

If a computer is left on for long periods of time, the monitor will get images burned into the screen. To prevent this from happening, you can select a screen saver that will constantly change to prevent images from burning into the screen. See steps below

1.2.1.1 Type "Screen Saver".

1.2.1.2 Select screen saver option desired

1.2.1.3 Adjust time delay

1.2.1.4 Select "Apply"

1.2.1.5 Select "OK"

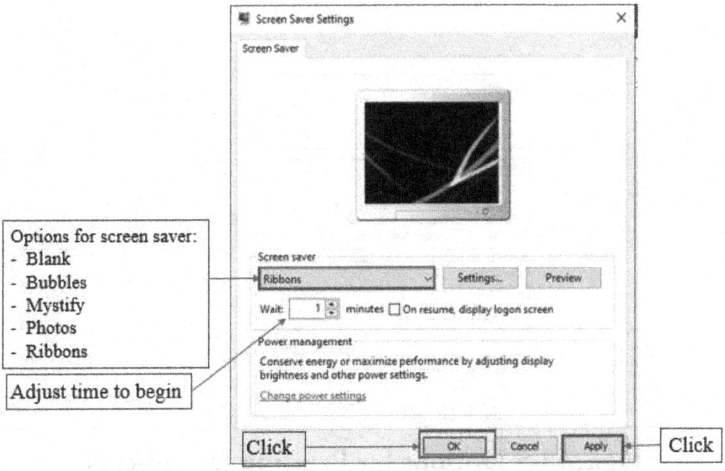

Figure 1.4 Screen Saver Display Properties

1.2.2 Printing Documents.

1.2.2.1 Options for Printing Documents

- Select "File Print"
- Dialog box depicted in Figure 1.5 will appear
- Options:
  - Print whole document, current page only or specify pages
  - Print one sided or two sided. Note for two sided option: Flip on **long edge** will print the pages so that you flip them like you would a **book**. Flip on **short edge** prints them so that your flip them like you would a **calendar**.

- ♦ Print portrait or landscape
  - o Select size of page: Letter 8.5" X 11"; Legal 8.5" X 14", Executive 7.25" X 10.25", Etc.
  - o Select Office default margins as needed.
  - o Select pages per sheet
- ♦ Select Print

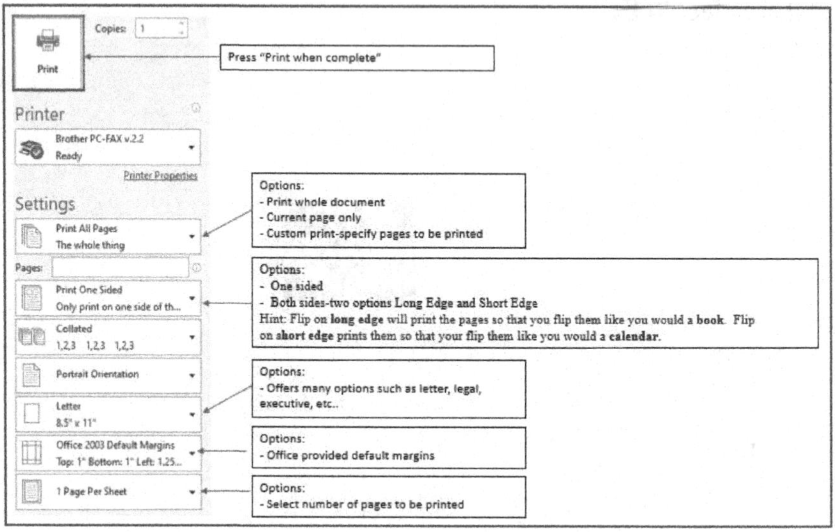

Figure 1-5 Options for Printing Documents

1.2.3 Accessories.

Most computers come with a variety of goodies that is just fantastic. When I first started to learn about computers, I was like a kid in a candy show when I learned about the accessories that are what Mister Mark calls "Freebies".

1.2.3.1 The Calculator.

Most computers come with a calculator installed. To find your calculator:
- Click "Start".
- Select "Calculator":

- Calculator. A normal looking calculator will appear with all the functionality we are used to. The calculator application includes various calculators and is also an excellent converter. Calculator capabilities are depicted in Figure 1-6.

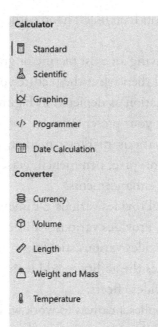

Figure 1-6 Calculator Capabilities

1.2.3.2 Playing and Storing music on Your Computer.

♦ Saving Music Albums to Your Computer:
  - Open Windows Media Player
  - Insert Music CD
  - Click the "Rip CD" Button
  - Program begins copying the CD's songs to your PC listing their titles in the Windows Media Player

1.2.3.3 Using Paint to Create Outstanding Graphics.

Paint is one of the most useful graphic tools and is provided at no cost on your computer by Microsoft.

- ◆ Click on Microsoft Icon in left hand corner, until you see "Paint 3D" and select.
- ◆ If you are modifying an exist picture or graphic, select "Menu" and "Insert" and then select the picture you want to insert.
- ◆ The Paint application as depicted in Figure 1-7 provides many ways to enhance your presentation as described below:
- ◆ Brushes. Uses various markers: marker, calligraphy pen, oil brush, water color, pixel pen, pencil, eraser, crayon, spray can, and fill to make enhancements.
  - ◆ 2-D Shapes. Provides various 2-dimensional shapes.
  - ◆ 3-D Shapes. Provides various 3-dimensional shapes.
  - ◆ Stickers. Provides various stickers.
  - ◆ Text. Provides the ability to add text.
  - ◆ Effects. Provides effects.
  - ◆ Canvas. Supplies a canvas to work with.
  - ◆ 3-D Library. Provides various 3-demensional pictures.

Figure 1.7 The Paint Program

1.2.3.4 Using Snipping Tool to Capture Images.

♦ The Snipping Tool is one of free applications provided by Microsoft. This by far is the best screen capturing application I have used.

♦ Click on search window at bottom left of screen and type "Snipping Tool". Suggest adding to tool bar since you will use this application many times.

♦ Open File you intend on capturing.

♦ Click on Snipping Tool application and click "New"

♦ Images will appear grayed out, place curse in top left and pull down and to the right.

   • A display of the image will appear. You have two options:

      ▪ Copy-simply click in the middle of image and select "copy"

      ▪ Save-File Save as, print or send to.

      ▪ To Save, you can save a desired location and save as Joint Photographic Expert Group (JPEG), Portable Network Graphics (PNG) or Graphic Interface Format (GIF). I prefer JPEG option because the files are smaller and offer very good graphics.

♦ The Snipping Tool and Microsoft PowerPoint are great when modifying JPEGs.

   • Open PowerPoint and select a blank presentation.

   • Insert JPEG file into PowerPoint and make modifications with PowerPoint such as adding text and other enhancements.

   • Recapture with the Snipping Tool as described above and continue to Save As your desired file name.

1.2.4 Other Good Information.

1.2.4.1 Determining Amount of Random-Access Memory (RAM).

♦ Click on search window at bottom left of screen and type "How much RAM do I have?" See Figure 1-8 for example of installed RAM.

Figure 1-8 Amount of RAM

1.2.4.2 Determining Computer Name.

♦ Click on search window at bottom left of screen and type "Computer Name". See Figure 1-9 for example of computer name.

Figure 1-9 Computer Name

1.2.4.3 Using Microsoft Excel to Keep Track of Financial Transactions.

- ◆ Open a blank Microsoft Excel spreadsheet
- ◆ Enter the following in each cell as follows:

Date	Check #	Description	Checks	Deposit	Balance

- • Modify the width of each cell as needed by clicking above top cell and pulling to the right.
- ◆ Left Click "View" and "Freeze Panes"
  - • Select "Freeze Top Row". The top row will remain visible regardless how long your spreadsheet becomes.
- ◆ Modify date column by right clicking above Column A-1 and select "Format Cells"
  - • Select "Date and then select date format you desire, for example: 11-Oct-21.
  - • Click "OK"
- ◆ Format columns D, E and F to currency by right clicking "Format Cells" and left click "Currency"
  - • Left click "Decimal Places" "2"
  - • Left click currency symbol desired for example "$"
  - • Left click "OK"
- ◆ Enter the current balance of your check book under "Balance". This should be identified as "F2" on the spreadsheet. I have entered $1,000.00.
- ◆ Enter your first withdrawal in cell "D3". I have entered $800.00.
- ◆ Enter your first deposit in cell "E-4". I have entered $1,200.00.
- ◆ Create a formula that will automatically calculate a balance for you.
  - • In column F3, type =(F2-D3+E4)
  - • Press "Tab" on keyboard.

- If desired you can place borders by:
  - Place curser in top left and pull to right and down to desired view.
  - Left click "Borders" and "All Borders"
- See Figure 1-10 for the checkbook spreadsheet created.

Date	Check #	Description	Withdrawal	Deposit	Balance
11-Oct-21					$1,000.00
11-Oct-21		Electric Bill	$800.00		$200.00
12-Oct-21		Deposit		$1,200.00	$1,400.00
					$1,400.00
					$1,400.00
					$1,400.00
					$1,400.00
					$1,400.00
					$1,400.00
					$1,400.00
					$1,400.00
					$1,400.00
					$1,400.00
					$1,400.00

Figure 1-10 Excel Checking Spreadsheet

2. The Electronic Filing Cabinet (Microsoft File Explorer)

Chapter two discusses how to use Microsoft File Explorer. I refer to File Explorer as the electronic filing cabinet. This chapter provides a description of the drives in your computer; how to create top level and sub-folders in your C-Drive also known as the hard drive; how to find files in File Explorer; copying files from the C-Drive and changing properties on files.

2.1 Description of Drives in Your Computer.

Your personal computer has many different compartments or drives where you can store information. The following section describes the hard drive (C-Drive), One Drive and the Portable Hard Drive. In some cases, this drive designation will vary depending on your computer's configuration. Figure 2.1 illustrates how the C-Drive, D-Drive, One-Drive and Portable Hard Drive appear in Microsoft File Explorer.

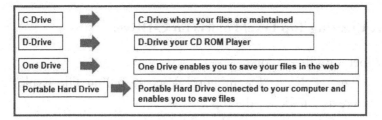

Figure 2.1 Computer Drives

2.1.1 The C-Drive or The Hard Drive.

The computers hard drive is where most of your information is stored. The hard drive is most commonly referred to as the "C" Drive. The C-Drive has lots of memory and is the primary means to store information.

2.1.2 The CD ROM Drive is normally your CD-ROM.

The CD ROM drive is normally used to play computer games, music CDs and so forth. It provides a means to gain access to large amounts of information.

2.1.3 One-Drive.

One-Drive is located on the web and provides a means to save your files. This is an excellent way to back up your files.

2.1.4 Portable Hard Drive.

Portable hard drives are also an excellent way to back up your work. Portable hard drives are connected directed to your computer.

2.2 Creating Folders in File Explorer.

File Explorer if properly used can help you keep a very accurate filing system for all of your files. It provides a means to create folders and sub-folders for all of your important information.

2.2.1 Creating Top Level Folders on C-Drive.

♦ Open up File Explorer.
  ♦ Left click on "Documents". You are telling File Explorer to create a folder at the top level.
    ♦ Right click and select "New Folder"
    ♦ Type "Creating a New Folder in File Explorer". See Figure 2-2 below.

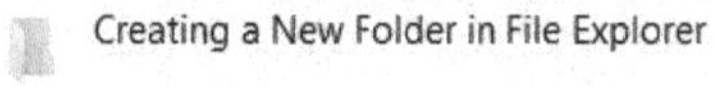

Creating a New Folder in File Explorer

Figure 2-2 Create a New Folder in File Explorer

2.2.2 Creating Sub-Folders.

In the above exercise we created a folder called "Create a New Folder in File Explorer". In this exercise you will learn how to create a sub-folder. Figure 2.3 illustrates the concept of sub-folder creation.

♦ Double Left Click on "Creating a New Folder in File Explorer".
♦ Right click and select "New Folder"
   ♦ Rename folder from "New Folder" to "Sub Folder 1 of New Folder in File Explorer".
♦ Right click and select "New Folder"
   ♦ Rename folder from "New Folder" to "Sub Folder 2 of New Folder in File Explorer".

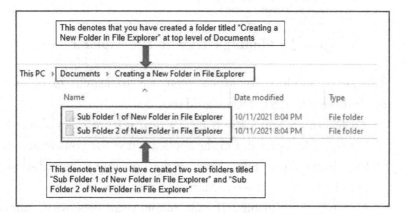

Figure 2.3 Sub Folders in New Folder in File Explorer

2.2.3 Using Quick Access to Maintain Most Used Folders for easy access.

♦ In File Explorer, simply drag and drop the folder into "Quick Access".

2.3 Finding Files with File Explorer.

On occasion all of us lose things. Murphy's Law happens to the best of us. I'm sure that Mr. Murphy would say this about lost files. If you happen to misplace a file, you will most likely misplace the one that you have been working on for weeks. If you happen to lose a file, File Explorer has an excellent way to find it.

♦ The search function for File Explorer is located at the top of the application as depicted in Figure 2-4 below.

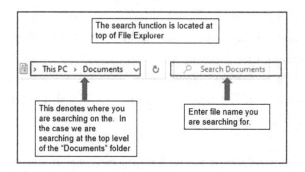

Figure 2.4 Finding Files with File Explorer.

♦ This handy window provides a great way to search. In order to search more effectively follow guidance below:
   ♦ All Microsoft applications have a neat feature. They show the last four files opened. On the application where you created the file, simply click "File". Look at the bottom of the pull-down menu and you will see the last four files opened.
   ♦ Naming conventions. If you name your files with names that you can remember, it is very likely that you won't lose them. Microsoft applications have lots of room to name your files. I name my files exactly what they are. For example, If I have created a Microsoft Excel file that has the balance of my checkbook, I would call this file "Checkbook Balance".
   ♦ Sometimes you may not know exactly what your file is called, but you have an idea. Let's use this file as an example. The name of this book is "Solving the Riddle of Microsoft". If I could only remember that the file name started with "Solving", I could still

find the file. You can use the "*" to substitute for the words you don't remember. Listed below is the process to follow:

♦ In the "Search" simply type "Solving*". The "*" helps look for all files that contain the work "Solving".

2.4 Copying Files.

Copying files is the most useful task that File Explorer provides. In order to fully understand what I am referring to; it is recommended that you review section 2.1 Description of Drives in Your Computer. In many instances, you will have to copy files from the C-Drive to One Drive, Portable hard drive and your USB (Universal Serial Bus) or thumb drive. In other instance you may have to copy files from one part of your C-Drive to another part of your C-Drive.

2.4.1 Copying Files From C-Drive.

♦ Open File Explorer. File Explorer is normally divided in half. The left half is showing the folder that you are opening. The right half depicts the contents of the open folder.

  ♦ Locate the folder and file you wish to copy from. Double click to open the file. To illustrate this, see Figure 2.5 below which shows:

  ♦ The folder "The Book" opened on the left.

  ♦ The contents of "The Book" on the right side.

♦ The file we are going to copy (blocked in red).

♦ The size of the file.

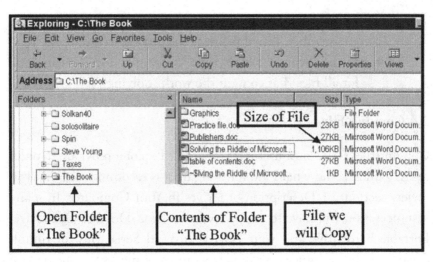

Figure 2.5 Description of Folders in File Explorer

♦ There are two ways to copy files:
  ♦ The best way to copy is what Mister Mark calls the drag and drop method. To an experienced computer operator this is something that is used constantly. To the unexperienced person, this can be frustrating. If you have problems with this. Microsoft developed a game that helps teach this technique. I suggest playing the card game solitaire to master this technique.
  ♦ The copy and paste are the best way to copy files that reside in the same folder. If you use the drag and drop method instead of the copy and paste, the file you intend to copy will move to where you intended to copy to. This can cause confusion.
♦ Open File Explorer.
♦ Right Click on file you wish to copy.
♦ Click "Copy"
♦ Locate the file you wish to paste the file into.
♦ Right click and select "Paste"

2.4.2 Changing Properties on Files.

In some instances, file properties need to be adjusted. See Figure 2.7.

♦ Right-click on file in Windows File Explorer.
♦ Left-click on 'Properties' in the contextual menu.
♦ Left-click on the value you wish to change and edit it.
♦ Left-click on 'Apply' or 'OK' to finish.

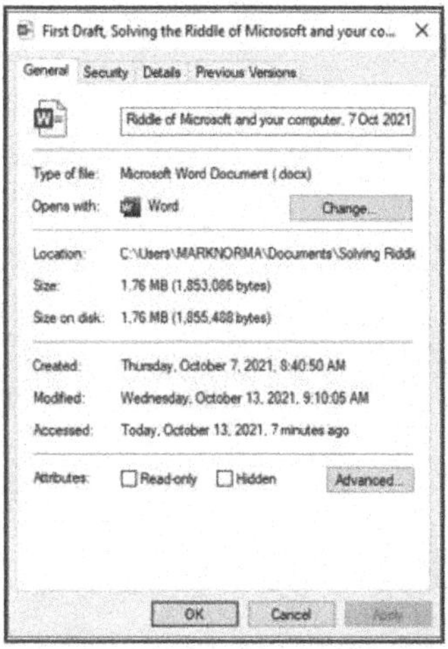

Figure 2.7 Modifying File Properties

3 Microsoft Word

Chapter three is the real meat of this book. It provides detailed information on the most useful Microsoft Word functions. You will learn how to use pull down menus to include (Find, Replace, Tracking Changes, Accepting or Rejecting Changes, saving files, Print Preview, Printing, inserting Headers and Footers); additional topics on cover pages, inserting blank pages, inserting page breaks, inserting tables and inserting pictures; next you will learn how to adjust margins, adjust orientation, adjusting size of paper, inserting columns, inserting page and section breaks, how to vertical line numbers; an in depth discussion concerning interactive table of contents; other useful tools include inserting symbols, inserting footnotes, inserting text boxes, inserting other files into Word, how to use Format Painter, description of formatting fonts and how to insert splits in Word.

3.1 Routine Functions of Microsoft Word.

3.1.1 Pull-down Menus.

3.1.1.1 Find Function.

The find function is a great tool to help find words and phrases in your document. Listed below is how this function works.

- Click "Find" at the top of the Word Application.
- A dialog box appears that provides a means to type the word you're looking for.
- See Figure 3-1.

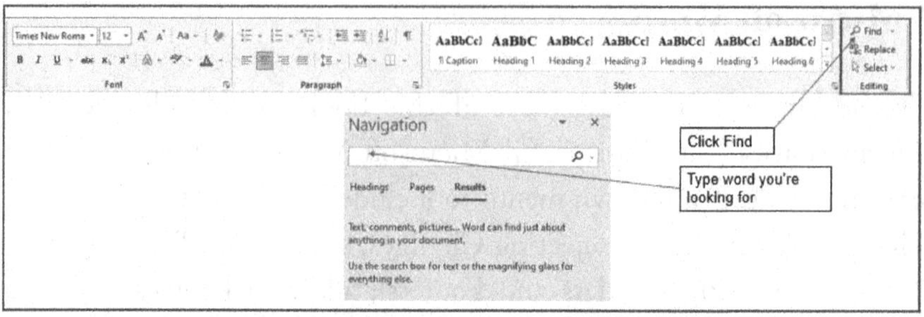

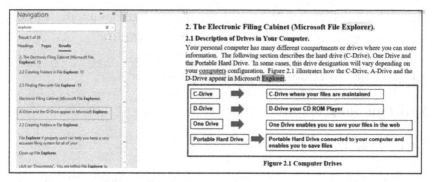

Figure 3-1 Finding words in Microsoft Word.

◆ I have typed the word "Explorer" in the navigation widow.

◆ All instances of the word "Explorer" are displayed for your review as depicted in Figure 3-2 below.

Figure 3-2 Results of Word Search

3.1.1.2 Replace Function.

The replace function is similar to the find function except it provides a means to replace words or phrases in the document all at once (globally) or one at a time.

◆ Click "Replace" at the top of the Word Application.

◆ A dialog box appears that provides a means to type the word you're looking to replace.

◆ There are three options: Replace, Replace All and Find Next. See Figure 3-3.

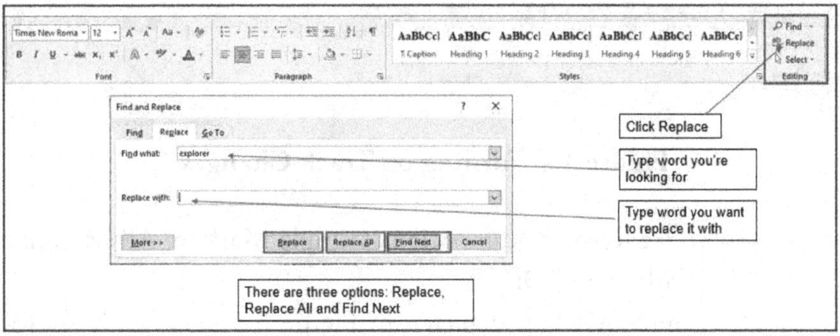

Figure 3-3 Replace Word Function

3.1.1.3 Tracking Changes.

Tracking changes is one of the most use tools that Microsoft Word has to offer. Imagine you are reviewing a document the old-fashioned way with paper. You have to go to the trouble of showing where errors by writing them out on the paper. Microsoft Word has a tool that does this function with more efficiency. The track changes tool many characteristics are highlighted below:

♦ In our first example, I'm going to show you how to change a word in a sentence. When the track changes tool is used, it shows the change to the document in two ways. It draws a vertical line to the left of the text and it also draws a horizontal line through the replaced text. The new text is indicated by underlining it. In my example, I originally typed "Sidney Crocket king of the wild frontier". Well, most people know that I surely must have meant "Davy Crocket King of the Wild Frontier". Follow steps below to learn how to use the track changes tool:
   ♦ In Microsoft Word application, select "Review".
      ♦ Left Click "Track Changes", two options will appear:
         ♦ Track Changes – select "Track Changes"
         ♦ Lock Tracking

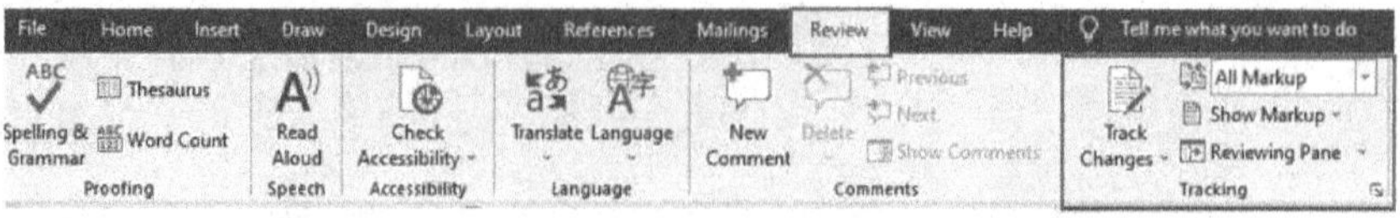

Figure 3-4 Turning on Track Changes

♦ There are four markup options (Simple Markup, All Markup, No Markup and Original.

  ♦ Simple Markup depicted in Figure 3-5 below only shows a vertical red line indicating where the changes are made.

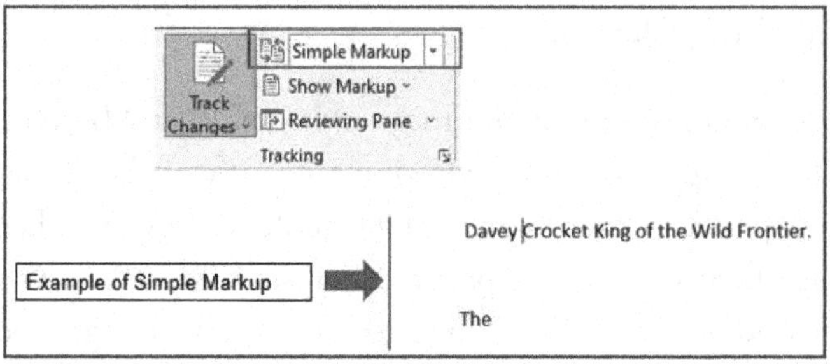

Figure 3-5 Simple Markup

♦ All Markup is depicted in Figure 3-6 below. All Markup shows more details of the changes made.

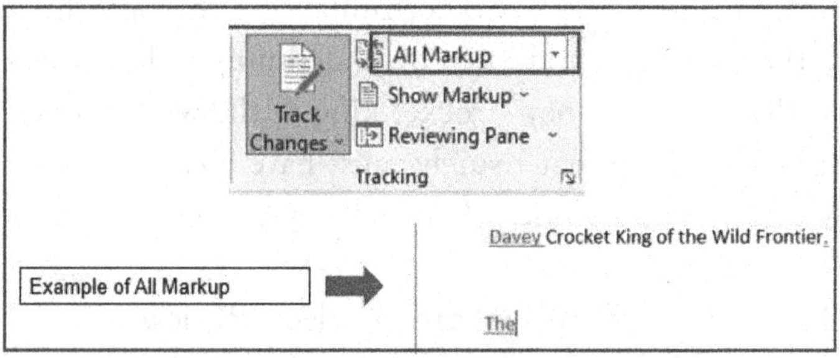

Figure 3-6 All Markup

♦ No Markup is depicted in Figure 3-7 below. No Markup shows how the document looks with all changes made.

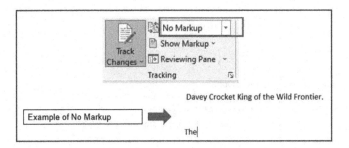

Figure 3-7 No Markup

♦ Show Markup provides other options which include: Comments, Insertions and Deletions, Formatting, Balloons and specific people.

♦ Reviewing Pane provides two options: Reviewing Pane Vertical and Reviewing Pane Horizontal.

3.1.1.4 Accepting or Rejecting Changes.

♦ When reviewing all comments on a document, there are two functions: Accept and Reject:

■ Accept provides options to Accept and Move to Next, Accept All Changes and Accept All Changes and Stop Tracking. See Figure 3-8.

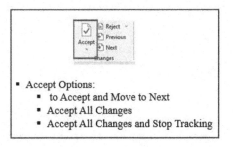

Figure 3-8 Accept Options

♦ Reject Changes provides options to Reject and Move to Next, Reject All Changes and Reject All Changes and Stop Tracking. See Figure 3-9.

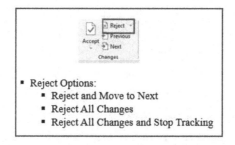

- Reject Options:
  - Reject and Move to Next
  - Reject All Changes
  - Reject All Changes and Stop Tracking

Figure 3-9 Reject Options

3.1.1.5 Saving Files Using the Save As Function.

There are many ways to save files. In this lesson we are going to discuss how to save files to a particular place. When saving files with the Save As function, you will learn how to place your word document into a folder created in File Explorer (Chapter 2).

- ◆ Click "File" pull-down menu and select "Save As". A dialog box of File Explorer will appear which provides a means to save the file in the desired location. A window will appear as depicted in figure 3-10.
  - ◆ If you need to find an alternate location, click "Browse" and navigate where desired.

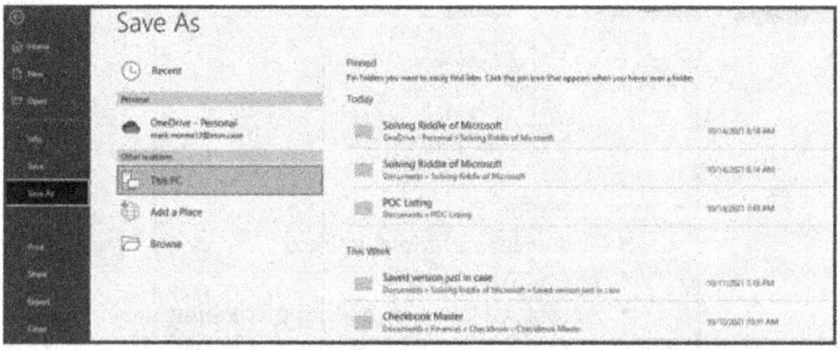

Figure 3-10 Saves as Function

3.1.1.6 Print Preview.

If you are unsure what your document will look like on a printed page, you can review it using the print preview function.

♦ Left click "File Print", a dialog box will appear which shows how the document will appear (Figure 3-11).

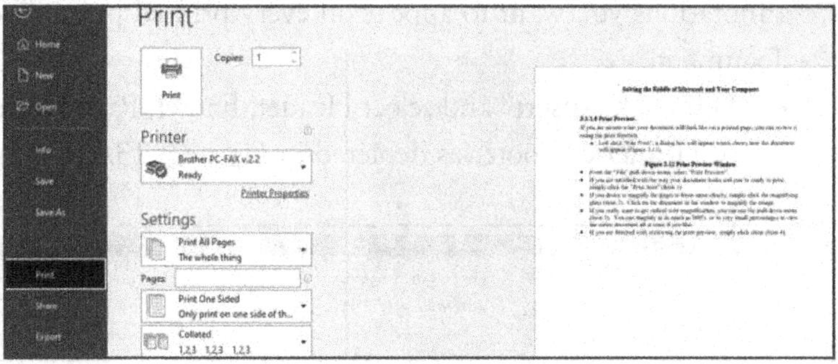

Figure 3-11 Print Preview Window

3.1.1.7 Printing.

The print pull-down menu is used when you want make special print requests to the printer. Figure 3-12 is a screen capture of the "Print" window which shows the various options you can use.

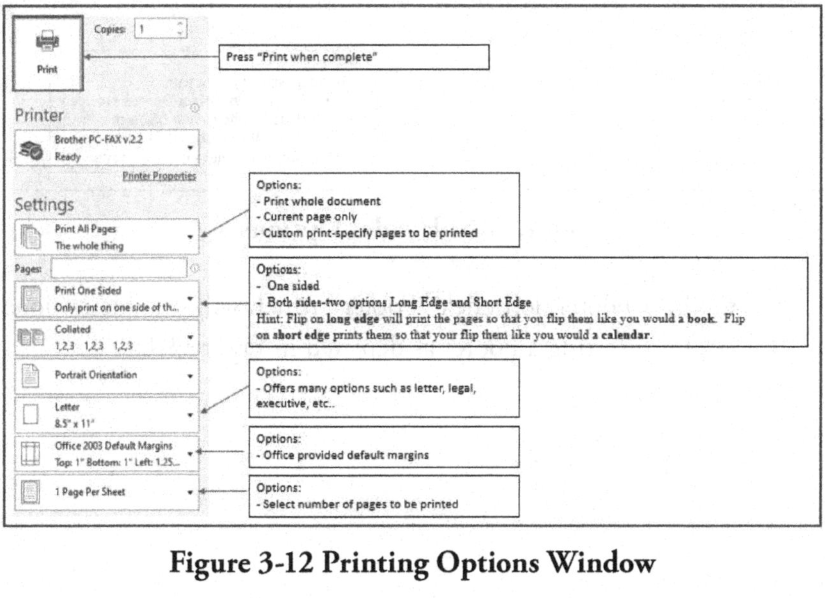

Figure 3-12 Printing Options Window

3.1.1.8 Inserting Headers and Footers.

♦ The Headers and Footers function are very useful for placing annotations you want to appear on every printed page of your document.

    ♦ Left click "Insert" and select Header, Footer, Page Number or Header & Footer as depicted in Figure 3-13.

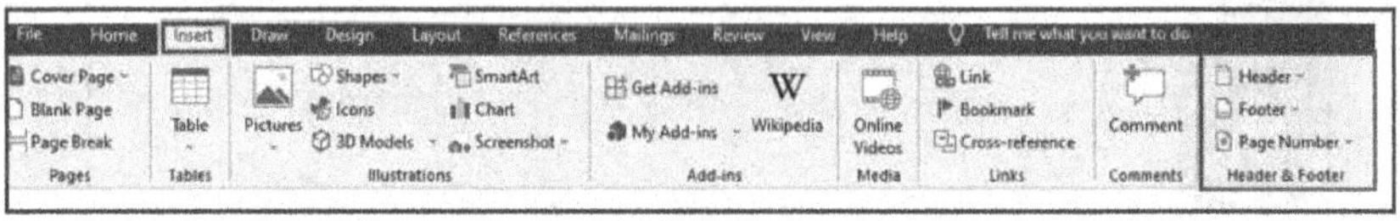

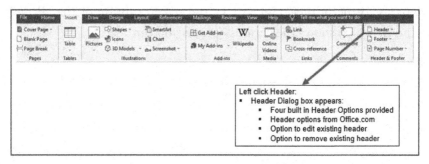

Figure 3-13 Headers and Footers Window

♦ Edit Header, left click "Header" which will provide options for inserting a header as depicted in Figure 3-14.

Figure 3-14 Header Options

♦ Edit Footer, left click "Footer" which will provide options for inserting a Footer as depicted in Figure 3-15.

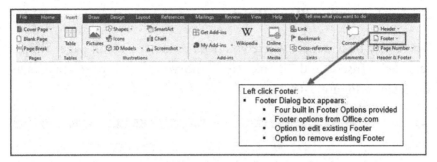

Figure 3-15 Footer Options

3.1.1.9 Inserting Additional Functions from Insert Pulldown.

Microsoft Word has more tool bars than you will ever need. It is good to learn what is available and how to obtain them just in case you might need these helpers. Left click "Insert" and tools associated will appear as depicted in Figure 3-16 below.

Figure 3-16 Inserting Additional Functions from <u>Insert</u> Pulldown.

3.1.1.9.1 Inserting Cover Pages.

Microsoft has developed many cover pages which can be edited to your needs. Left click "Insert" and select "Cover Page" as depicted in Figure 3-17 below.

Figure 3-17 Cover Pages.

3.1.1.9.2 Inserting Blank Pages.

There may be instances where you need to insert a blank page. Simply left click "Insert' and "Blank Page" and your blank page appears as depicted in Figure 3-18.

Figure 3-18 Inserting Blank Page

3.1.1.9.3 Inserting Page Breaks.

There may be times you need to insert a page break. Left click "Insert" and "Page Break" as depicted in Figure 3-19.

Figure 3-19 Inserting Page Breaks

3.1.1.9.4 Inserting Tables.

Left click "Insert" and "Table".
- Several options will be offered.
  - A grid will appear, left click and pull to the right to select the number of rows and columns.
  - Insert an Excel Spreadsheet
  - Quick Tables which Microsoft has created
- Other functionality:
  - **Deleting Cells.**
    - Highlight the cells you wish to delete.
    - Click the "Table" pull-down menu and select "Delete". The cells highlighted cells disappear.
  - **Merging Cells.** Merging cells comes in handy if you are building a table that has rows which have different numbers of columns.

- Highlight the cells you wish to merge.
- Click the "Table" pull-down menu and select "Merge". The highlighted area will become one cell.

♦ **Splitting cells.** Splitting cells comes in handy if you need to create additional columns in a row.
  - Highlight the cell you wish to split.
  - A split cells window will appear.
  - Select the number cells you wish to have.
  - Click OK.

♦ See Figure 3-20.

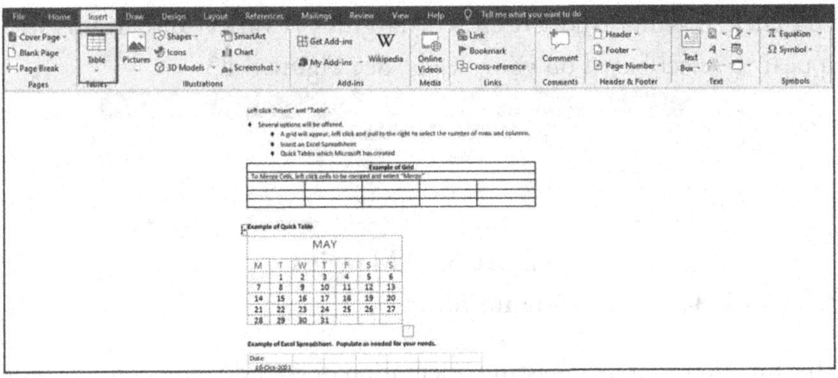

Figure 3-20 Inserting Tables

3.1.1.9.5 Inserting Pictures.

When inserting pictures use JPEGs since they are significantly smaller than Bitmaps. Paragraph 1.2.3.4 provides guidance on using Snipping Tool and Power Point to capture images.

♦ Left click "Insert" and "Pictures" and locate the picture you need inserted into your document. You will have two choices:
  ♦ "From this device" which means it's filed on your C-Drive
  ♦ On Line Pictures
♦ Left click image and select "Insert"

Figure 3-21 Inserting Pictures

3.1.1.10 Using Layout to Adjust Document.

The Layout provides a means to adjust your document to desired settings. Left click "Layout" as depicted in Figure 3-22.

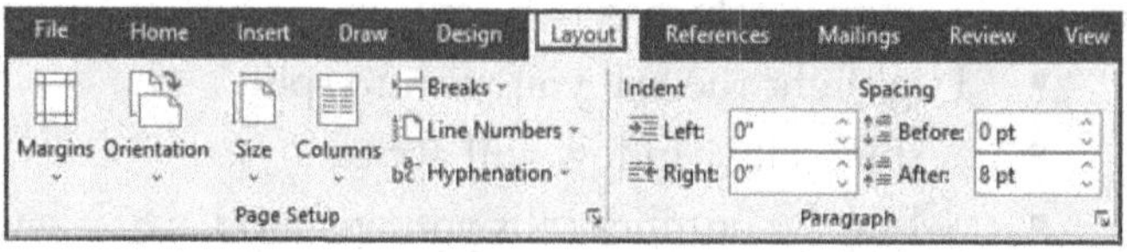

Figure 3-22 Layout Functions

3.1.1.10.1 Adjusting Margins.

Left click "Layout" and left click "Margins". A variety of margins will appear to select based on your needs. See Figure 3-23.

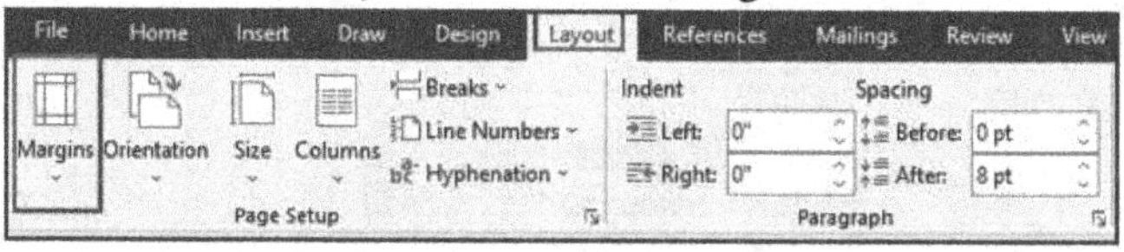

Figure 3-23 Margins

3.1.1.10.2 Adjusting Orientation.

This function enables adjusting orientation of your document to Portrait or Landscape. Left click "Layout" and left click "Orientation", select Portrait or Landscape from pull down menu. See Figure 3-24.

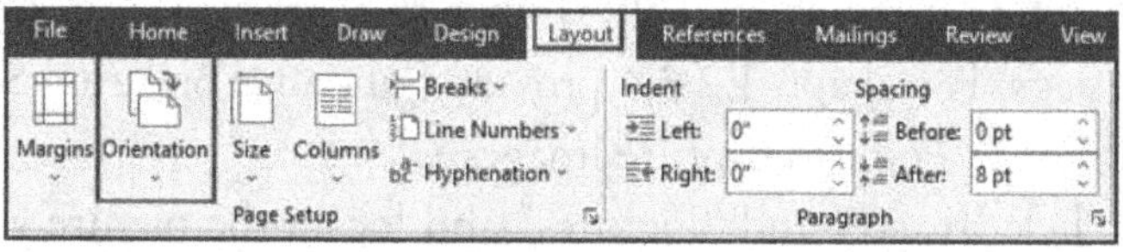

Figure 3-24 Adjusting Orientation

3.1.1.10.3 Adjusting Size of Paper.

This function provides a means of selecting various paper sizes. Left click "Layout" and left click "Size". Select the paper size that suits your needs.

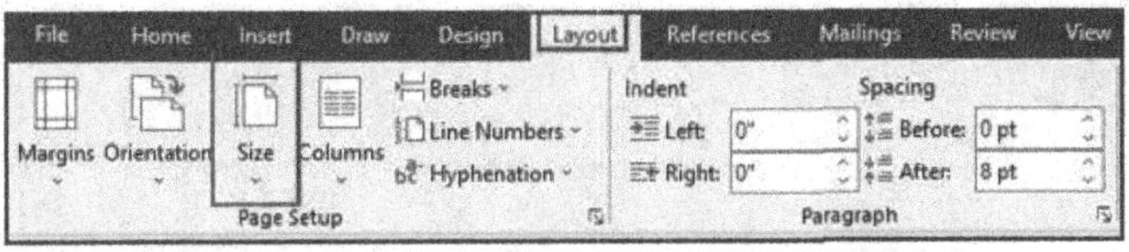

Figure 3-25 Selecting Paper Sizes

3.1.1.10.4 Inserting Columns in Microsoft Word.

This function provides a means to insert columns. Left click "Layout" and left click "Columns". There are half dozen templates created by Microsoft. I have selected two equal columns to illustrate the functionality. See Figure 3-26.

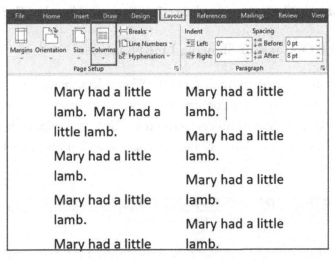

Figure 3-26 Inserting Columns

3.1.1.10.5 Options for Inserting Page and Section Breaks.

Left click "Layout" and left click "Breaks" which provides a pull-down window with options depicted in Figure 3-27. Note: Information provided obtained from Microsoft Help Topics.

Information in this table obtained from Microsoft Help topics	
Options for Page Breaks	
Page	Marks the point at which one page ends and next page begins.
Column	Indicates that text following the column break will begin in the next column
Text Wrapping	Provides means to separate text around objects on web pages, such as caption text from body text
Options for inserting Section Breaks	
Next Page	Starts the new section on the following page. Often used with chapters.
Continuous	Starts the new section on the same page. This type of section break is often used to change the number of columns without starting a new page.
Even Page	Starts a new section on the next even-numbered page.
Odd Page	Starts a new section on the next odd-numbered page.

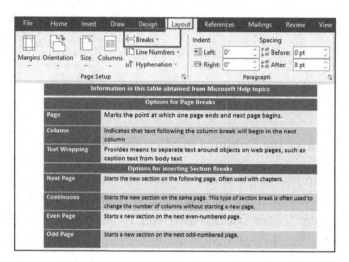

Figure 3-27 Options for Inserting Page and Section Breaks

3.1.1.10.6 Options for Showing Line Numbers.

Showing line numbers in Microsoft Word documents helps action officers who are staffing documents to other organizations because it provides vertical line numbers so discrepancies can be identified more accurately. Left click "Layout" and left click "Line Numbers". See Figure 3-28.

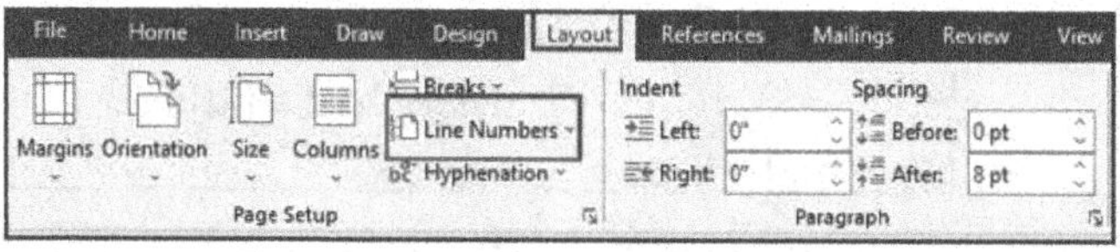

Figure 3-28 Options for Showing Line Numbers

3.1.1.10.7 Adjusting Vertical Spacing Above and Below Text.

Microsoft Word provides a means to adjust the vertical space above and below text. Left click on "Layout" and adjust vertical spacing before and after text as depicting in Figure 3-29.

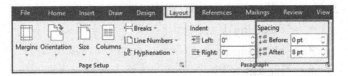

Figure 3-29 Adjusting Vertical Spacing

3.1.1.11 Inserting Interactive Table of Contents.

The creation of an interactive table of contents is one of the most useful tools that Microsoft Word has to offer. It provides a means to move throughout a document without having to search through each page. This is also one of the more difficult functions to master. *The Theory of Why Difficult Tasks are a Blessing. The good thing about hard things is there are not many people who know how to do them. That is why they pay the players for the New York Yankees so much – they are more talented than the average Joe. Once you have mastered the means to create a document with an interactive table of contents, you will be head and shoulders above the rest of the crowd.* Solving the Riddle of Microsoft and your computer has an interactive table of contents. Microsoft has created tutorial on creating a table of contents. To view the Microsoft tutorial for Interactive Table of Contents, left click "File" and select "New". Left click on document titled "Insert your first Table of Contents". See Figure 3-30 below.

Figure 3-30 Inserting Table of Contents Tutorial

♦ Honestly, Microsoft's tutorial confused me, so suggest following my instructions.
　♦ Open a blank version of Microsoft Word.
　♦ Leave page 1 blank for now.

- ♦ Add the following as separate lines
  - ▪ "Heading 1"
  - ▪ "Heading 2"
  - ▪ "Heading 3"
  - ▪ "Heading 4"
- ♦ Left click "Home" and you will see Heading 1 through Heading 6 above styles. See Figure 3-31.

Figure 3-31 Screen Capture of Heading 1 through Heading 6

- ♦ Let's go to the document you just created:
  - ♦ Left click "Home" button.
  - ♦ Highlight "Heading 1"
    - ▪ Click on Heading 1.
  - ♦ Highlight "Heading 2"
    - ▪ Click on Heading 2.
  - ♦ Highlight "Heading 3"
    - ▪ Click on Heading 3.
- ♦ On Page 1 of the document:
  - ♦ Left click "References" and select "Table of Contents". See Figure 3-32 below.

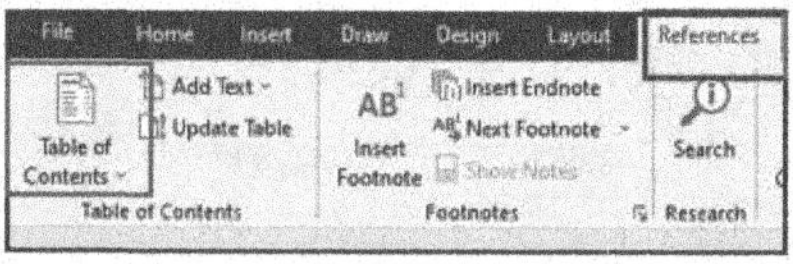

Figure 3-32 Inserting Table of Contents

- ♦ The Table of Contents with Heading 1, Heading 2 and Heading 3 appears as depicted in Figure 3-33. The Table of Contents is formatted so the different headings are indented. The page numbers of each heading are on the right side.

Contents

Heading 1 1

Heading 2 1

Heading 3 1

Figure 3-33 Table of Contents

- Now that the Table of Contents has been created, you can begin adding additional headings to the document and see how easy it's to update the Table of Contents:
  - Add the following Text to main body of the document:
    - Heading 1—Additional Information and Left Click "Home" and "Heading 1"
    - Heading 2—Additional Information and Left Click "Home" and "Heading 2"
    - Heading 3—Additional Information and Left Click "Home" and "Heading 3"
    - **Note: Make sure you highlight text before clicking Heading 1, Heading 2 and Heading 3**
  - Click on "Contents" at top of document and select "Update Table"
    - Left click "Update Entire Table" and everything you marked will be incorporated into the Table of contents as shown in Figure 3-34 Updated Table of Contents.
    - Note: In some instances, the "Update Table" function will be absent. If this happens, Left click "References" and select "Update Table".

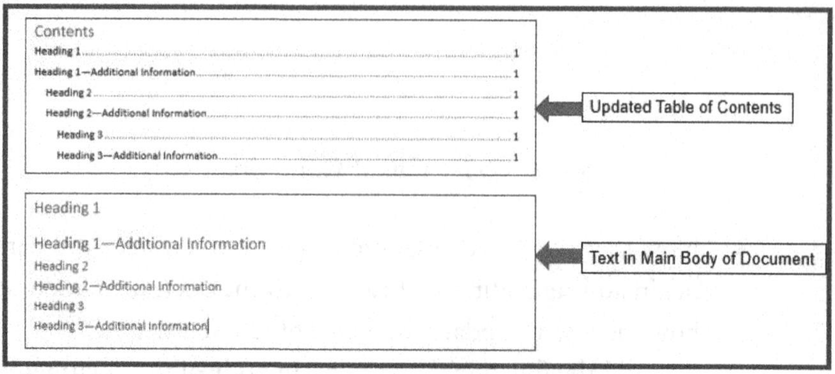

Figure 3-34 Updated Table of Contents

3.1.1.12 Other Useful Tools.

3.1.1.12.1 Inserting Symbols.

There are times when you may need to insert a symbol that is not present on the keyboard. In this instance, Microsoft provides a way to insert rarely used symbols. Left Click "Insert" and select "Symbols" as depicted in Figure 3-35. You will have option of selecting the symbol you need to insert into your document.

Figure 3-35 Inserting Symbols

3.1.1.12.2 Inserting Footnotes.

If you are doing a paper that requires the use of footnotes, Microsoft Word can insert the footnote in the correct format. See Figure 3-36.

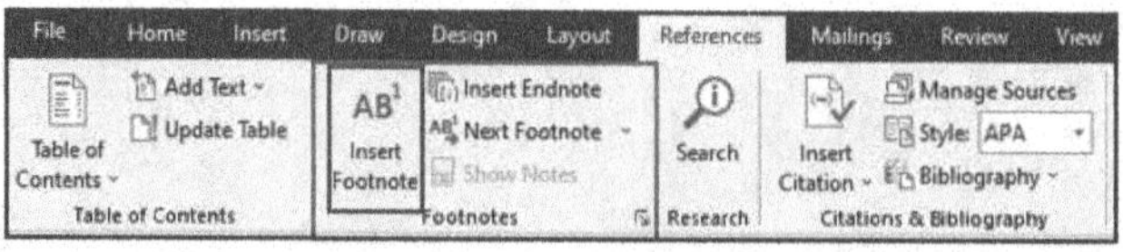

Figure 3-36 Footnote and Endnote Window

- Place your cursor in the document where you wish to make the foot note.
- Left click the "References" and select "Footnote". The Footnote and Endnote window will appear.
  - If you desire to insert a footnote on a particular page, click "Footnote". Two things will happen:
    - A small number will appear in superscript to the left of what you are making reference to.
    - A number will appear at the bottom of the page. Word will draw a horizontal line above the entry.
    - The rest is up to you. Refer to the publication manual that applies to your activity and type your footnote in the prescribed format.
  - If you desire to insert an endnote at the end of the document, click "Endnote".
    - Word will automatically go to the last page and place your endnote. As with the footnote option, Word will place the endnote in the correct format. The rest is up to you by referring to your publication's manual.

3.1.1.12.3 Inserting a Textbox.

Textboxes can add emphasis to a document. The text is enclosed in a rectangle to draw the reader to its contents.

- Place your curser where you want to place the text box and Click the "Insert" and select "Textbox". Microsoft offers quite a few options to pick from. Left click desire option and it will appear in your document. See Figure 3-37.

Figure 3-37 Inserting Textbox

- Start typing inside the box. The text will automatically do a carriage return. See below for an example of a text box (Figure 3-38).

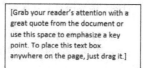

[Grab your reader's attention with a great quote from the document or use this space to emphasize a key point. To place this text box anywhere on the page, just drag it.]

Figure 3-38 Text Box Example

- The unique thing about a text box is that it is completely separate from the rest of your document.
  - If you want to move it, move your mouse over the text box until you see a "+", then left click.
    - Click on the border and hold the left mouse. Move your mouse, the text box will follow you like a little dog.
    - If you need to modify the size of the text move, click on the small circles on the sides of the text box and pull.
    - If you want to modify the text in the text box, simply click inside the text box until you see your cursor blinking inside. The functionality is the same as regular word documents except it is inside a small text box.

3.1.1.12.4 Inserting a File into Microsoft Word.

- Open the first document.
- Place the cursor where you want the second document to be inserted.
- From the Insert tab, Text group, click on the down arrow next to Object and choose Text from file. See Figure 3-38.

Figure 3-39 Inserting Files into Word

- Select the file to be inserted.
- Click on Insert.

3.1.1.12.5 How to Use Format Painter.

Format Painter is one of the most useful tools you will find in Microsoft Word. In some instances, you will need to change the properties of text in word. Highlight the area of the document that contains correct properties, Left click "Home" and select "Format Painter" as depicted in Figure 3-40.

Figure 3-40 Format Painter

3.1.1.12.6 Formatting Fonts.

When creating documents in Microsoft Word, there may be times that you may need to modify the font of particular parts of your document. This section will teach you how to modify fonts. To modify a font, it must be highlighted before attempting these modifications. Left click "Home" and Font Group is depicted in Figure 3-41.

Figure 3-41 Font Groups

3.1.1.12.6.1 Modifying Fonts.

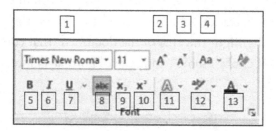

Figure 3-42 How to Modify Fonts

- See below for tips on modifying below.
  - Annotation 1- click down arrow to select style desired and font size.
  - Annotation 2- Increases font size.
  - Annotation 3 – Decreases font size.
  - Annotation 4- Changes selected text to uppercase, lowercase or other common capitalizations
  - Annotation 5-Change to Bold
  - Annotation 6-change text to Italicize
  - Annotation 7-underlines text
  - Annotation 8-strike through text
  - Annotation 9-types very small letters just below line of text
  - Annotation 10-types very small letters just above line of text
  - Annotation 11-Adds some flair to your text, such as shadow or glow
  - Annotation 12-makes your text pop out by adding bright color
  - Annotation 13-Changes text font color

3.1.1.12.7 Inserting a Split in a Word Document.

Splitting a Microsoft Word document provides a means to view different parts of the document at the same time. Left click "View" and select "Split" as shown in Figure 3-43.

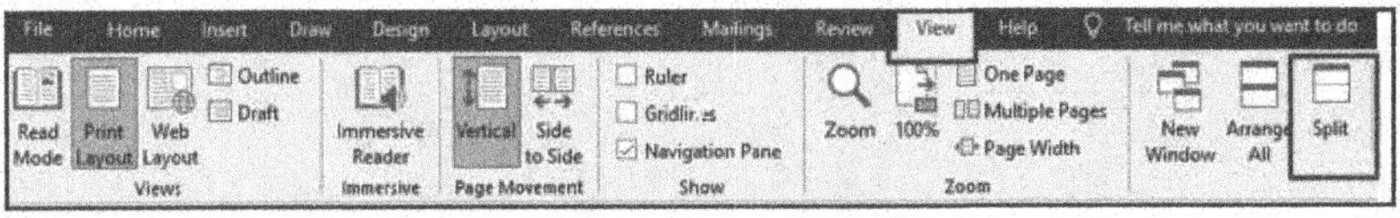

Figure 3-43 Splitting a Word Document

Printed in the United States
by Baker & Taylor Publisher Services